Perspectives

Patrick Broe

Copyright © 2021 Patrick Broe
All rights reserved

Dedication

These poems come from a lifetime of experiences and relationships. They are each dedicated to the people or events which inspired them but the catalyst for creating the collection was the tragic death of my big brother, Brendan. He played a pivotal role in many, many peoples stories and whilst he was on it, he made the world a better place. I owe huge thanks to my family and many friends who have encouraged and supported me throughout this project. A special thanks to our wonderful sons, William and Mark. You make my world a hopeful place.

Contents

Introduction 6
Perspectives 7
97 Curzon Street 8
Mother Earth 11
Our May 13
A Shared Big Bang 15
Pride 17
Our Kid 19
The Virus of Our Age 21
Twin Star 23
Too Late to Say 25
A Fatal Combination 26
Chances Are 27
Commitment 29
Could You Live Here? 30
Foster Parents 32
Dragon Slayer 33
Confessions 35
Memory 36
Star 38
The Fight of Your Life 39
When the Truth Becomes a Lie 42
Why Me? 44
Twenty-One 45
The Tides of Love 46
My Gift 47
A Father's Blessing 49
Casualties 50
Clay From the Stars 51

All is Not Loss 52
Covid Time 54
Dreamers 56
Each Day I Die a Little More 58
Home 59
Living with Loss 60
M 62
A Line for All Seasons 63
The Human Condition 64
When I Was a Runner 65
Thanks 67
Awakening 68
Friends 71
Closing Perspectives 72
About the Author 75

Introduction

Perspectives is a collection of poems about life, its triumphs and challenges, ups and downs. There is no instruction manual for living, we find inspiration and role models where we can. No matter what choices you make or whichever paths you take you will experience joy and pain, success and failure, pride, and shame. These are all part of our lives, and we must learn to accept and even embrace them. All of these will pass. The impact that they have on your life is down to perspective. Perspectives are viewpoints and we can all choose our own. Indeed, we can change ourselves and our perspectives throughout our lives. These poems reflect my interpretations of many life events common to us all. I hope they resonate with you and renew your faith in yourself and humanity.

Perspectives

The way we feel
Determines what we see
Defines how we interpret
Our world
Emotions colour our mood

The same circumstances
Can discourage or inspire us
Depending on how they
Are viewed
We relate pain or glory
To our personal story
As if we're the
Star of the show

Feelings and emotions
They're only thoughts
And notions
Concepts so easily changed
When you feel
You can't make it
Change your viewpoint
Get creative
Make your feelings work
For you
not against

97 Curzon Street

An old workshop shed
A cellar for coal
An outside loo
It froze in the winter
Wasn't fit for so many
The house with a yard
But it's where
Our family lived
Where my most precious of precious
Blossomed and grew

From the smell of
Sunday breakfasts
To our dad's
Sad departure
The weddings
The lodgers
The treasured front room
Our mam singing
San Francisco
The welcome for everyone
Till the immersion wire
Blew

97 was our sanctuary
Our own special nursery
The place where
The Broes lived
Our forever home

I Wanted to Change the World

I wanted so
To change the world
I wished
My life would matter

To make
Others believe
That they
Might achieve
That their
Origins don't
Really matter

To invest
In each other
As
Sister and brother
No limits
To what
We can
Strive for

When we
Stoke up
The fire
Of another's
Desire
We light up
Their passion
And purpose

When this life
Nears its end
We may measure
Our impact
By the
Lives we have
Touched and
Made better

Mother Earth

Our home
Has come from
A mixture
Of
Many things
Some heavy
Some light

Some liquid
Some solid
All attracted
To this speck
By gravity

She
Has weathered
Many storms
She was almost
Torn apart
Giving birth
To her
Daughter
Moon

She
Has raised many
Families
Seen many
Species
Come and
Go

We
Are the
Current
Alpha Ones
But
We
Abuse
Her
With abandon
Burn her
Riches
Choke her
Air

She
Will endure
Our
Majestic
Mother
Earth

Alas
we
Will be
Gone
Back to
Our mother
To roam
Her realm
As dust
Once more

Our May

She gave me life
She showed me courage
She filled my world
She taught me love

Her name was May
And she stamped
It on our hearts
Our mother
May

She struggled
All her life
She didn't
Seek fame or fortune
She managed and
Made do
Stretched a pound
Till it snapped

She battled
On with courage
When she lost
Her darling
Paddy
Frightened
Heartbroken but
Still in the game

She raised us
Twelve
Gave us our start
Then
Just as life's
Struggles
Should have been
Past
We lost our precious
May

If lives were
Measured by
the love
They inspire
My mam
Was
Rich beyond kings

A Shared Big Bang

All of this can't have come
From nothing
There is so very much
It must have come from
Somewhere

But
Where?
How?
Can all that we see
All that we feel
All that we are
Have really
Come from
Nowhere
Nothingness?

Maybe
It's like
Meeting your soulmate
Or
The birth of your
Baby
Once it happens
Nothing
Is ever
The same
Again

Your universe
Expands
Life becomes bigger
Brighter
Filled with colour
And light

You struggle
To remember
A time before
Can a butterfly
Recall
Being a larva?

Nothing
Comes from nothing
All that is
And all that may be
Comes from
Potential
And our lives are
Filled with
It

Pride

Pride can swell
Your heart
To bursting
And
Pride can shrink
Your heart
To breaking

Let others
Fill your heart
With pride
As you watch
Their struggle
And triumph

Be kind
To yourself
And others
Being the only
One
Makes you
The lonely one

Celebrate your success
But not
In a boastful
Proud display
Share your success
Use it
As a beacon
To guide those
Still searching
For the way

If you share
Yourself
With others
At the end
Of this road
Your heart
Will be full
To bursting
Not
Shrunken
And empty

Our Kid

It's hard to grow up in the shadow of a giant
All you can do is hang on to their coat tails
The best you can do is follow behind
A candle in the blazing sun

That giant was my brother
Somehow, he filled the earth
With warmth and light
His eyes and smile
Focused on you
Laser like
When caught in that beam
You couldn't help but
Feel
Valued
Priceless

His impact on so many
Lives was
Mountainous
Like a mountain
You could see him
When you were down
In the depths
He was comfortable in
His own skin
And generous enough
To invite you in

It's not hard to grow up in the shadow of a giant
He taught me to be me
That riches come
From sharing

I thought he stood alone
But
He made the world
His family
Now we all
Mourn
His loss

The Virus of Our Age

As we continue our conquest
Of planet earth
Pushing all other
Life forms
To the brink
Making space
For us to live in
We encounter
New and deadly foes
All conquest has its
Cost

Our arrogant entitlement
And ignorance of
Consequence
Propel us on our way
We consume all
That we see
With no thought of
Tomorrow

But our victims
Harbour deadly spores
Legions of lethal
Cargo
What we devour
Devours us
Predator becomes prey

Too late
We harness reason
Science and necessity
Wreak miracles from havoc

What lesson have we
Learned from this
That may leave us
Here tomorrow

Twin Star

I met you on the way up
Our stars ascending
Your light and mine
Sparkled synchronised bonded

For a time
We shone brightly
Together
A fabulous new
Gemini
In the heavens

Our reign
Was sweet and bright
As we swept
Through
Time and space

Until you were
Trapped
By the
Gravity
Of a powerful
And dreadful
Force

The dark vortex
Tore you
From me
An unquenchable
Thirst
Stretching then
Swallowing
Your light

When a
Binary
Splits
Two
Does not
Become
One

One
Becomes
Zero

Too Late to Say

I climbed the stairs
I'd said goodnight
I heard a scream
I felt the fright
My dad poleaxed
A dreadful sight

I sprayed his meds
I prayed for help
I watched him die
My mam came back

She called his name
She held him tight
He could not hear
He'd lost his fight

A week later
We were told
He'd died
our world collapsed
We cried and cried

The years have passed
Our lives progressed
We've all grown up
Our paths digressed

If I could have
That night once more
I'd tell my dad
I love him
Now and
Forever more

A Fatal Combination

When responsibility
Meets denial
It is the collision
Of an unstoppable force
Meeting
An immovable object

Responsibility
Craves ownership
Whilst
Denial
Seeks escape

If neither meet
They
Co-exist, without
Enmity or judgement
But
When they clash
Both
Get smashed
To pieces

Chances Are

Chances are
That I may
Meet you
Again
In the salon

I might hear
Your laughter
On the wind

How could we
Have been
So close
Now
So very
Far apart

Chances are
So fickle
We had
The chance
To
Be
Together
But
We never
Had the
Chance
To
Say
Goodbye

When you were
Real
Solid
I took
Your presence
For granted
Now
You are
Wisps of memory
I strain
To
See you
Clearly

Chances are
Choices
Opportunities
To write
A new history

While I
Draw breath
I will
Take my chances
Grateful
For the
Lives
I have shared

Commitment

The greatest sin
We can permit
Is in our
Failure
To commit

To ourselves
Our lives
Our dreams our friends
Without commitment
All things end

The greatest gift
We can receive
Comes when we
Commit
To what we love
From that connection
Our lives are touched
We change the world
The beauty in our
Souls unfurled
Commitment Reveals
What we don't see
There's no us or them
There's only we

Could You Live Here?

When our government's
Settle on action
To destroy
Some other souls
Home

We are moved
By the speakers with passion
Enraged by injustices
Done

We advance
And we flatten
The fabric on which
They rely
Their schools
homes
And hospitals
Flattened from out
Of the sky

Our mercy is
Boundless
As we surgically strike
Killing
Men women children
So that they might
Know freedom
Their shackles
We break

And when the dust settles
Their histories
Gone
We rebuild their country
A brand spanking
New one

If you were returned
To the site
Of your loss
Of lives loves
Shared memories
Even your mosque

When governments claim
No alternative to war
Ask yourself one question
Could you live here?

Foster Parents

What a wondrous gift
To sponsor
A life
A life
Without hope
Or purpose

To offer
A stranger
A chance
Of success
When their nature
Signposts only
Distress

To delight
When their plight
Gives way to insight
When their
Voice from within
Insists that
They win

When the shackles
Of hopelessness
Are released
By resourcefulness

When the love
We all need
Is sown
As a seed
The rewards are
To great
To be counted

Dragon Slayer

If I could slay the Dragon
Who breathes fire from every flagon
I would drive my sword
Clean through its heart
But this beast that devours
Preys on those whose willpowers
Are prone to accede not to fight

I can't be a substitute
To defeat this brute
I can only argue
That you must fight it
For the price of defeat
Is too great to concede
To survive you must
Face it and smite it

The fire that it breathes
Consumes all your needs
Severs every human connection
The smoke and the flame
Choke off where you came
Fill your life with contempt
And deception

Though I'd spill my last drop
To rescue you from this trap
There is no blow
That I can deliver
To defeat this beast
From you
must come at least
A decision to live
Not to wither

Dragons are myths
And the power they enlist
Is nothing but self-delusion
For God's sake wake up
Take your life back
Don't give up
Escape this senseless
Oblivion

Confessions

As a child I was introduced
To the concept of confession
It promised forgiveness
For all my sins
Accessible redemption

As time went by
My faith declined
Replaced by sure suspicion
To share my darkest secrets
Was to expose myself
Make me vulnerable

Despite my distrust
Of confession as a sacrament
I find that all my writings
Projects and relationships
Have been attempts
At self-confession

We need no go between
Our own
Forgiveness washes us clean
Honesty sets us free
We must redeem the whole
Not just the best parts

When we share ourselves
With our kin
We open the doors
Let them in
We confess who we are
And accept theirs too
Without judgement
With love and compassion

Memory

For as long as I live
All the people I've loved
Are right here
accessible to me
They remain bright and clear
They can always be near
Through the wonderful lens
Of memory

As our time marches On
The path we've walked along
Is littered with streetlights
Of memories
We know we've been here
And who we've been near
Thanks to our personal
Biographer
Memory

The joy and the pain
They have both
Been our gain
From pages and chapters
Written with others
They've developed the plot
Fleshed out characters
Helped when we were lost
Those beautiful
Sisters and brothers

As we think back
On them
Let's remember again
That we appear
In other peoples
Stories
So, let's pick up
The pen
Write the next line with them
Leave them access to
Wonderful memories

Star

If I can leave a thought behind
To spare another's anguish
Don't waste your time
Trying to prove your worth
To others
Find value and pride
Where your heart resides
Never fear that your
Virtues don't matter

The light that you bring
Comes from passions within
Burn with faith
In the cause that you champion

While we all bear regrets
The worst are the chances
We've wasted
Until our voice fades
We must raise it
Demand
A hearing not
Lip service posted

Make your time here count
Trust your instincts
Don't doubt
Believe that we all
Make a difference

Make a stand
Run your race
Make your mark
On this place
No fear no regrets
You're a star

The Fight of Your Life

We would all be hammered
To the canvas
By a terminal diagnosis
And kept there for a good long count

As we haul ourselves
Back up
On the ropes
We might Marshall our defences
Prepare to return the fight
But we always
Knew that this life
Would one day
Come to a stop
As they say
No one gets out
Of life alive

We might count our many blessings
Try to return
The love we have received
Try to exit with Grace
Show that hope can be our
Legacy

But addiction
Doesn't announce
It's devastating
Presence
It makes itself
Your pal
Convinces
That you're in this fight
Together
Addiction is always
By your side

Addiction is jealous
Your relationship
Must be kept
Quiet, exclusive

At first
It steals your life
Moment by moment
By the time
You realise
That you are in
The Fight of your life
It has gutted you
Separated you from
Yourself

You might try
To battle it
Alone
But it
Knows all your moves
And persuades
What's the point?

But this
Cancer
Can be beaten
You can
Reclaim your life
You'll need help
And support
To believe
No fighter
Makes it
On their own

Love and care
For your
Self
You are never
Really alone
Take strength
And hope
From others

No one seeks
Addiction
It is just as random
And
Just as deadly as
Cancer

When the Truth Becomes a Lie

When the truth
Becomes a lie
The word
Becomes a sword

When we sacrifice
Other beings
For
Our faith
In holy meanings

When we
Follow
Any prophet
Whose only goal
Is profit

We throw reason
On the
Fire
To bring light
To our
Desire

But no
Light can pierce
The darkness
Of our chosen
Moral blindness

When our thirst
For right
Denies
Another's plight
Right becomes
Wrong

If we lived
By perfect
Rules
And none were ever broken
There would be
No need
Of salvation

We are all shipwrecked
By the folly and certainty
Of our own beliefs
Our only hope
Of rescue
Is to recognise
The truth
And work together

Forgive our cruelties
Forget our arrogant
Righteousness
Recognise our shared
Humanity
Reconnect what we have broken
Rediscover what we have lost
Remove the poison
That the wound
May heal

Why Me?

Why me?
Why do I
Have to suffer?
I don't deserve this
It's not fair
This shouldn't
Happen to me

When life
Doesn't fit
With our
Game plan
When the worst
That can happen
Just did

We can shout
Foul
And demand
A concession
We can blame
Everything that we
See

But
The truth is
That all life
Is random
There simply is
No guarantee

From
Conception to grave
Every breath that
We breathe
Is against all the odds
It's
Not free

Twenty-One

When I look back
To twenty-one
My life was full of promise
The million lives
That I might lead
By degrees came down
To one

The vast array
Of paths to walk on
The choices pondered
Voices heard
Till all too soon
My time was gone

I'm not complaining
No time for blaming
For each of us
It is the same
Whilst we consider
The script gets written
Our life stories bear our names

Now you
Our youngest
Have reached your
Twenty first
I wish you all
A father wishes
A treasured and beloved son

I pray through life
You'll always find
A reason for living
Never lost
Never question your own value
Write your story
Spend your time
Don't count the cost

The Tides of Love

It hits you in waves

Sometimes just shifting the earth
Beneath you
Sometimes scooping you up and bodily
Pounding you onto the beach

There are spells when you
Want to walk beside it
Keep it at bay

There are eons when you need
To be submerged in it
Wrapped up in oblivion

It leeches salt from your pores
And your eyes
Till you're
Floating in brine

The worst are the doldrums
When you feel no motion
Only galactic silence

You reach to the heavens
Beseeching your moon
To show its face

But these tides of love
Flow from
Within you
Beats of your heart

The love you've shared
And thought you'd lost
Swells and recedes
But you'll never be apart

My Gift

When you feel alone unloved unlovable
And so very unavailable and lost
Especially to yourself
Remember me

If I am permitted to give
But one gift
To you
I give you
Myself

It is all I possess
And
All we may possess
And from that
Comes its
Value

We spend our
Entire life
Becoming

But we begin our
Journey
With accepting

Acceptance of
Our self
Is the beginning
Of loving
Our self
And this we
Must do
In order to
Know love

When you learn
To love yourself
You
Light a beacon
That guides
Your way

You will grow
You will change
But always
You
Will
Shine

When the light
Is lost inside you
I give you
My light
Till
Yours
Shines through

A Father's Blessing

When I can't be with you
Please know that I long to be there
Every dream comes true in your presence
All my greatest achievements are there

Please remember
The times that I held you
Know I loved you
Without question or price

Feel the strength of our bond
When you need me
No quarrel to poison
Or blame

You're the love
That my life
Leaves as witness
To my story
My journey
My name

Casualties

Our hearts used to beat together
I grew inside your shell
We began my life together
My security was your smell

When I fell, you'd always lift me
Make me believe I could excel
I used to know that your smile meant
sanctuary
All in my world was well

Now you're consumed by a thirst
Called alcohol
Captivated by its spell
If I could break its hold
I'd shatter it
Rescue you from your own private hell

You will always be my mother
Have a special place in my heart
If I could make you believe
In yourself once more
Find the courage to make
A fresh start

Clay From the Stars

The scars which we carry
Are the clues to
Our story
We can cover
The shaping but
Can't undo the scraping
Once changed we can never
Go back

Our orbits
Propel us
Smash and repel
Us
Caught up in an
Intricate dance
From these cosmic clashes
Explosions, dispatches
From violence and mayhem
We are made

Life breaks and repairs
Us
Constantly shapes
Us
A journey of
Perpetual change

The clay of our scars
Comes from
The demise of the
Stars
The stitches that
Bind us
Connect and
Define us
Are the patterns
That make us
Who we are

All is Not Loss

How do you let go
When you're hanging on
For dear life
How do you throw away
What cost so much
To make your wife

How do you untie
The knots
That bind you tight
What went so wrong
Which was
So right

How do you learn
To try once more
When the prize
Is lost
Beyond restore

There's no one
To blame
No call for shame
Just tragic
Evolution

All is not loss
For a while
What bliss
No regrets
For chances
Taken

To have breathed
That air
The highest Vista
We were there

The pain of losing
Is part of choosing
To share yourself
With another soul

Covid Time

This time we've had
Has been so sad
And all
Because of Covid

It has shut us off
From all we love
Our families
Our friends
Our futures

Some of us
Have lost so much
We struggle for
Perspective
Our sense of
Who we are
Has dimmed
We long to find
Our purpose

Covid has exposed
Us to
The fault lines
In
Our nature
Arrogance selfishness greed deceit
Seem amplified
And shame us

Yet catastrophe
Brings forth
Champions too
The salt
Our world is made of

They exemplify
What we all can be
They challenge
Our inertia

From captain Tom
To the mighty Tony Hudgell
Our world
Is full of local heroes

To make this world
A better place
Demand a just tomorrow
Let's take our race
To a kinder place
Out of this vale
Of sorrow

Dreamers

What an extraordinary gift
To be a human being
When you see what we've done
How far we've come

In our short history
We've achieved so much
From inventing the wheel
To walking on the moon

We can comprehend
The universe
Eradicate diseases
Maybe
Rescue our earth

No one doubts
We can deal
With climate change
It's our prevarication
I find so strange

When we work together
For a single purpose
The entire resource of humanity
Focused on a sole objective
Imagine the miracles
We might achieve

Every day new wheels
Need invention
Distant worlds
Await discovery
And exploration

With each successive generation
We break new ground
Expand horizons
Increase our knowledge
Realise potential
Bring dreams to life

Each Day I Die a Little More

Each day I die a little more
My iron resolve
Slowly eroded
To rust

Life's disappointments
Just mount up
To heights
I dare not
climb

I find no comfort
In battles won
No outlet
For my rage

Though time is short
I must prevail
I have so much
To do here

Give me your hand
To help me
Out
I know
That I can
Make it

From these dark days
I will emerge
Renewed
In my conviction
That where life is
There
Hope survives
And
I
Shall be
It's witness

Home

Home
The place where our heart lives
Where our ship was launched from
We long one day
To return
Once youthful stale familiarity
Now yearns for sight of home

The place we found our bearings
Offered security and love
From a corner of mams
Nightgown
To the planets and the stars above

We would venture ever further
Still keeping
Home in sight
Till we learned to bring it with us
Roam as far as we might

Time and tide
They wait for no one
Soon our home's
No longer there
Yet
It stays with us
For always
Built with
Tender loving care

Living with Loss

At first
Living with loss
Is recovering
From shock
The emptiness
Left where your
World was

Slowly you
Explore the space
Try to retrace
Where your balance
Your future
Your joy was

As the scars
Dry and seal
You pray God
You might heal
But you know
Something's changed
Forever

Part of you
Is bound tight
To the one
Who's now lost
Your life
Witness
To their
Once vital
Presence

Like the moon
And the stars
We carry the scars
Of all those
Who've touched our world
We display the craters
Of our movers and shakers
Yet continue our path
Through the cosmos

M

If I had only shared your burden
If I could've only eased your pain
You lost your innocence too early
You felt that you must be to blame

You learned to sell yourself
As currency
Your worth discredited
By shame

The guilt you bore
Right to your core
For someone else's outrage
Destroyed your sense
Of self-respect
Removed any hope of refuge

Your life too short
Chose to abort
If I could only
Tell you
Though you're at peace
Final release
How much I really
miss you

A Line for All Seasons

In spring we played
Drank lemonade
Thought everything was
Forever
Our youth was gold
To be bought and sold
There would always
Be tomorrow

Summer came and changed
The game
We planted roots
And grew
The life we spawned
Promised
A new dawn
Our dreams could all
Come true

As Autumn slowly
Ambled in
Our days grew
A Little shorter
Our families grew
Moved to pastures new
The pulse of life
Seemed slower

Now winter's here
It seems so clear
The things we did
Don't matter
What we remember
With joy and tears
Are the people
Times and
Banter

The Human Condition

Through all our longing
To belong
We desperately seek favour
From some special group
Or tribe
We yearn for permission
To say
I'm home

Though down each new
Blind alley
Along those
Rocky roads
We find we lose
Our bearings
We're heading further
From home

The journey is not out there
It's inside
We must roam
Discover who
Your self is
Make a path
All of your own

There is room for all
And sundry here
No price for
Admission
Or special
Condition
If you're human
You're one of
Our own

When I Was a Runner

When I first ran
I thought I could fly
The miles
The gradient
No problem

I would escape
From my day
Fly
Far, far away
Where the air
Was rich
And heady

From the side of
Thorpe cloud
To the top
Of
The fan
And across the
Peaty
Moorland

Now I must
Be content
To slog
Slowly and bent
On the roads
Of my
Beautiful island

As I Survey the World We've Made

As I survey the world we've made
I shiver to see such
Shamefulness
After all the sacrifices
Our parents made
We revel in selfish
Indulgences

Our morals for sale
Corruption wholesale
No excuse to feeble
To cling to

Our leaders they scoff
Like pigs round a trough
While we tutt and say:
"Who shall we vote for"

Oh, let us
Seize power
Away from this shower
Build the world
That our ancestors
Fought for

When our children look back
Let's not shame them
With lack
Of morality
Accountability
And duty
Let's fill them with pride
We didn't let down
The side
We stood up for justice
And truth

Thanks

You made me smile today
And I forgot
To say thanks
I took a moment
To catch a breath
And realised
I forget a lot

To all those heroes
Who picked me up
When I was down
For all those
Little kindnesses
That eased my days
Thanks

For writing lines
In my story
For letting me
Reflect in your glory
Thanks

For allowing me in
To share the pain
For standing by me
When I drove you insane
Thanks

To almost everyone
I've ever met
To all of you
I owe a debt
I can't repay the gifts
You've given
I can't find the words
How much you meant
But I can say
Thanks

Awakening

At last
You have woken
From your
Nightmare

I didn't
Think
You ever
Would

I thought
My
Vigil over
And
Waited
Empty
For the
End

While you
Were
Gone
I
Searched
For myself
But
Found
Only shadows

Finally
I
Accepted my
New
Shrunken
Self
And
Looked ahead
Without
You

I turned
For one
Last
Look
Across
The void
Between
Us

I found
You
There
Beside me
Longing
Hoping
But
No longer
Lost

I reached
Out
Touched you
And
We both
Awoke
The nightmare
Retreating
The bonds
Of
Love
Returning

May we
Never
Lose
Our way
Again
Until
We
Close our
Eyes
For the final time

Friends

If I could take your hand
Make you understand
How much your pain
Is my pain

The hurt you feel
So sharp and real
Cuts you off
Breaks all human connection

When you're crippled and lost
Desperate for support
Let go
Let me sustain you

Rest your weight on me
I'll carry you
You'll see
Just how much
You matter to me

To make journeys end
We all need
A friend
Someone who loves us
And forgives us

We can weather
Any storm
Get through the darkness
See the dawn
If we put our
Faith and trust
In each other

Closing Perspectives

As we trace our way
Through the story
Seeking key lines
Or passages
Details that light up
Our part

We unconsciously edit
The plot line
Find meanings
Not there
At the start

We find patterns
We've followed
Lines that we've
Crossed
Looking back
From a distance
They converge
On this spot

But our plot lines
Are only perspectives
We are only the star
In one plot
Even our greatest
Distance
Can't give us vantage
Our search for meanings
Obscures the plot

Our story
Had no one
Beginning
With our
Final line
It won't end
It's a journey
We all take
Together
Each step
Echoed
Again, and again

In the vacuum
Of time
Nothing's past
The present is
All that there is
But
In the vastness of
Space
Nothing's lost
Every sight every sound
Continues
When we look
At the stars
We see where
We once were
And where
Our ghosts one day
Will be

About the Author

Patrick was born in Derby, England. His parents were both from Dublin and he is one of twelve children. He is married to Peggy and they have two sons, William and Mark. He has over forty years of experience as a hairdresser, twenty-six as a martial arts instructor and worked in various roles within the personal development sector. He is fascinated by and has a wealth of experience in developing relationships.

Patrick has written many training programs covering Hairdressing, martial arts, and personal development. He published his first book, *Relationships R Us*, in 2017. Patrick has spent the last 30 years living and working in the Outer Hebrides.

Printed in Great Britain
by Amazon